French
FOR
DUMMIES
Audio Set

by Zoe Erotopoulos

BICENTENNIAL
1807
WILEY
2007
BICENTENNIAL

Wiley Publishing, Inc.

French For Dummies® Audio Set

Published by
Wiley Publishing, Inc.
111 River St.
Hoboken, NJ 07030-5774
www.wiley.com

Copyright © 2007 by Wiley Publishing, Inc., Indianapolis, Indiana

Published by Wiley Publishing, Inc., Indianapolis, Indiana

Published simultaneously in Canada

For general information on our other products and services, please contact our Customer Care Department within the U.S. at 877-762-2974, outside the U.S. at 317-572-3993, or fax 317-572-4002.

For technical support, please visit www.wiley.com/techsupport.

Wiley also publishes its books in a variety of electronic formats. Some content that appears in print may not be available in electronic books.

Library of Congress Control Number: 2006939443

ISBN: 978-0-555-03703-4

Manufactured in the United States of America

SKY52218055-7491-4173-BE25-1CF5354FFD5D_032922

WILEY

About the Author

Zoe Erotopoulos holds an M.A., M.Phil, and Ph.D. in French and Romance Philology from Columbia University in New York City. She has also studied in Aix-en-Provence, at the Sorbonne, and at the Ecole Normale Supérieure in Paris. Her teaching experience in French ranges from elementary to advanced-level courses including literature and theater. Dr. Erotopoulos's area of expertise is 17th-century French Theater. She has taught at a number of institutions including Columbia University, Reid Hall in Paris, and Trinity College in Hartford, Connecticut. For the past 15 years, she has been teaching in the Department of Modern Languages and Literatures at Fairfield University in Fairfield, Connecticut. Dr. Erotopoulos lives in Connecticut with her husband and three children.

Publisher's Acknowledgments

We're proud of this book; please send us your comments through our Dummies online registration form located at www.dummies.com/register/.

Some of the people who helped bring this book to market include the following:

Acquisitions, Editorial, and Media Development

Senior Project Editor:
Tim Gallan

Acquisitions Editor:
Lindsay Lefevere

Senior Copy Editor:
Elizabeth Rea

Technical Editor: Language Training Center

Audio Produced by:
Her Voice Unlimited, LLC
(hervoice@iquest.net)

Media Project Supervisor:
Laura Moss-Hollister

Media Development Specialist: Kit Malone

Editorial Manager:
Christine Meloy Beck

Media Development Manager:
Laura VanWinkle

Editorial Assistants:
Erin Calligan, Joe Niesen, David Lutton

Cartoons: Rich Tennant
(www.the5thwave.com)

Composition Services

Project Coordinator:
Kristie Rees

Layout and Graphics:
Stephanie D. Jumper, Erin Zeltner

Proofreaders: Susan Moritz, Mildred Rosenzweig

Wiley Bicentennial Logo:
Richard J. Pacifico

Publishing and Editorial for Consumer Dummies

Diane Graves Steele, Vice President and Publisher, Consumer Dummies

Joyce Pepple, Acquisitions Director, Consumer Dummies

Kristin A. Cocks, Product Development Director, Consumer Dummies

Michael Spring, Vice President and Publisher, Travel

Kelly Regan, Editorial Director, Travel

Publishing for Technology Dummies

Andy Cummings, Vice President and Publisher, Dummies Technology/General User

Composition Services

Gerry Fahey, Vice President of Production Services

Debbie Stailey, Director of Composition Services

Table of Contents

Introduction

● ●

*T*hroughout the world, people regard the culture of France not only with high esteem but also with a sense of romance. The French language has a certain . . . *je ne sais quoi,* right? And doesn't just about everything sound better when you say it in French. With global travel easier than ever — for business road warriors, students studying abroad, and vacationers — understanding and speaking a little French doesn't have to be a chore when you have *French For Dummies Audio Set.*

About This Audio Set

French For Dummies Audio Set enables you to quickly familiarize yourself with the French language and begin communicating on a basic level with other French speakers. By listening to the hour-long CDs and following along in this booklet, you can set your own pace and introduce yourself to the topics that interest you. CD1 gives you the very basics of French; CD2 covers the structure of the language; and CD3 presents the language in real-world situations.

By the way, you can play the CDs in this audio set on any CD player, so you can listen in your car, on your home stereo, or on your computer.

Conventions Used in This Audio Set

So that you can easily follow along with the CDs and this booklet, I stuck to a few conventions:

✔ The lessons numbers in this booklet correspond to the track numbers on the CDs. So Lesson 1:3 corresponds to the third track of CD1, and Lesson 3:10 corresponds to the tenth track of CD3. Track 1 of each CD is an introduction, which you can skip if you want.

✔ On the CDs, the narrator presents words and phrases in English. Then a native French speaker says the words and phrases in French. A pause gives you time to say the word or phrase yourself. Then the French speaker repeats the word or phrase a second time and pauses to give you another chance to repeat the word or phrase.

✔ French terms are set in *italics* in the booklet to make them stand out.

The Tip icon indicates helpful information that aids in your understanding of pronunciation, grammar, and other elements of the language.

Foolish Assumptions

In producing this audio sest, I had to make some assumptions about who you are and what you know:

✔ You know no French — or if you took French in school, you don't remember very much of it.

✔ You're not looking for a product that will make you fluent in French; you just want to know some words, phrases, and sentence constructions so that you can communicate basic information in French.

✔ You don't want to memorize a bunch of boring grammar rules.

✔ You want to have fun and learn a little bit of French at the same time.

How This Audio Set Is Organized

The booklet is divided into four parts, and the first three parts each correspond to one of the CDs.

> ✔ **CD1: The Basics:** This CD presents greetings, indispensable words and phrases, useful questions, an overview of numbers and dates, and other basic French information.

> ✔ **CD2: The Nitty-Gritty Language Structure:** This CD introduces nouns, verbs, adjectives, articles, and other parts of speech so that you can develop an understanding of how French sentences are put together.

> ✔ **CD3: Real-World Situations:** On this CD, you're introduced to vocabulary, phrases, and sentences that you will find useful while working, traveling, eating out, shopping, banking, and more.

> ✔ **Mini-Dictionaries:** The fourth part of this booklet contains a handy French/English dictionary and English/French dictionary for quick reference on the go.

Where to Go from Here

Pop any of the CDs into your player and start listening and repeating. CD1 is the place to begin if you know nothing about French. If you know a little bit (or just feel adventurous), check out the Table of Contents and jump to any lessons that catch your eye, even if they happen to be on CDs 2 or 3. Listen to the tracks that interest you, and discover French at your own pace. Enjoy.

The 5th Wave

By Rich Tennant

Introduction and Overview of CD1: The Basics

* *

*O*n Disc One, you start off with the pronouns, followed by introductions and greetings, common words and phrases, and finally words and phrases that you just can't live without.

Personal Pronouns and Formalities

• •

Personal pronouns

I	*je*
you (S)	*tu*
he	*il*
she	*elle*
we	*nous*
you (S/Formal or Plural)	*vous*
they	*ils* (M or mixed group); *elles* (F)

Use *j'* instead of *je* if the verb begins with a vowel or a mute h.

 Use *tu* with people you know well, like members of your family, friends, children, and peers. Use *vous* with people you don't know well and with your superiors, like your boss, your teacher, or elders. Although *vous* can also mean plural you, it can also refer to one person when used formally.

Formalities

Mr./Sir	*Monsieur*
Mrs.	*Madame*
Miss	*Mademoiselle*

Saying "Hello" and "Goodbye"

Greetings

hello; hi (Informal)	*salut*
hello; good morning	*bonjour*
good afternoon	*bon après-midi*
good evening	*bon soir*
good night	*bonne nuit*
How's it going?	*Comment ça va?*

 Use *bonne nuit* only if you or someone else is going to sleep.

Goodbyes

goodbye	*au revoir*
goodbye (Informal)	*salut*
see you soon	*à bientôt*
see you in a minute	*à tout de suite*
see you later	*à plus tard*
until next time	*à la prochaine*
see you tomorrow	*à demain*
see you next week	*à la semaine prochaine*

see you on Monday	_à lundi_
Have a good day!	_Bonne journée!_
Good luck!	_Bonne chance!_

Aside from a few exceptions, final consonants aren't pronounced in French. You pronounce a consonant only if it's followed by a vowel.

Saying and Replying to "How Are You?"

How are you? (Informal) — *Comment vas-tu?*

How are you? (Formal) — *Comment allez-vous?*

How's it going? (Informal) — *Ça va?*

It's going well. — *Ça va bien.*

Everything is going well. — *Tout va bien.*

I'm fine, thank you. — *Je vais bien, merci.*

I'm very well. — *Je vais très bien.*

I'm not doing very well. — *Je ne vais pas très bien.*

I'm so-so. — *Je vais comme-ci, comme-ça.*

And you? (Informal) — *Et toi?*

And you? (Formal) — *Et vous?*

Introducing Yourself and Talking about Where You're From

● ●

*I*f you're meeting someone for the first time, it's always more polite to use the *vous*, or formal, form. Of course, you can use the *tu* form when speaking to children even if you're meeting them for the first time. The following questions are posed in both the *tu* and *vous* forms so that you can practice both forms.

What's your name? (Informal)	*Comment t'appelles-tu?*
What's your name? (Formal)	*Comment vous appelez-vous?*
My name is Olivier.	*Je m'appelle Olivier.*
I'm Caroline.	*Je suis Caroline.*
What's your first name? (Informal)	*Quel est ton prénom?*
What's your first name? (Formal)	*Quel est votre prénom?*
What's your last name? (Informal)	*Quel est ton nom (de famille)?*
What's your last name? (Formal)	*Quel est votre nom (de famille?)*
My last name is Nadal.	*Mon nom de famille est Nadal.*
Delighted.	*Enchanté.*

Delighted to make your acquaintance.	*Enchanté de faire votre connaissance.*
It's a pleasure to meet you.	*C'est un plaisir de vous rencontrer.*
Likewise.	*De même.*
What country are you from? (Informal)	*De quel pays es-tu?*
What country are you from? (Formal)	*De quel pays êtes-vous?*
I'm from the United States.	*Je suis des États-Unis.*

Lesson 1:6

Indispensable Words and Phrases

* *

Pleasantries

yes	*oui*
no	*non*
please (Informal)	*s'il te plaît*
please (Formal)	*s'il vous plaît*
Thank you.	*Merci.*
Thank you very much.	*Merci beaucoup.*
You're welcome. (Informal)	*Je t'en prie.*
You're welcome. (Formal)	*Je vous en prie.*
It's nothing.	*Il n'y a pas de quoi.*
Excuse me.	*Excusez-moi.*
Please repeat.	*Répétez, s'il vous plaît.*

Asking for help

Help!	*Au secours!*
information	*renseignements*
police	*la police*
emergency	*urgence*
doctor	*médecin*
accident	*accident*

The definite articles (*the*) in French are

- ✔ *le* for masculine singular nouns
- ✔ *la* for feminine singular nouns
- ✔ *l'* for either masculine or feminine singular nouns that begin with a vowel or a mute h
- ✔ *les* for either masculine or feminine plural nouns

Places

the city	*la ville*
the country	*le pays*
the train station	*la gare*
the airport	*l'aéroport*
the hospital	*l'hôpital*
the hotels	*les hôtels*
the church	*l'église*
the restaurants	*les restaurants*
the bathroom	*la salle de bains*

 The indefinite articles (*a* and *an*) in French are *un* (masculine) and *une* (feminine).

People

a man	*un homme*
a woman	*une femme*
a boy	*un garçon*
a girl	*une fille*

a child	*un enfant* (M); *une enfant* (F)
a father	*un père*
a mother	*une mère*
a son	*un fils*
a daughter	*une fille*
a brother	*un frère*
a sister	*une sœur*
a husband	*un mari*
a spouse (M)	*un époux*
a wife	*une femme*
a spouse (F)	*une épouse*
a friend (M)	*un ami*
a friend (F)	*une amie*

Useful Expressions and Phrases

* *

Excuse me.	*Excusez-moi.*
I don't understand.	*Je ne comprends pas.*
Can you repeat that?	*Pouvez-vous répéter?*
Could you speak slower?	*Pouvez-vous parler plus lentement?*
I don't speak French very well.	*Je ne parle pas bien français.*
Can you translate for me?	*Pouvez-vous traduire pour moi?*
Do you speak English?	*Parlez-vous anglais?*
Yes, I speak English.	*Oui, je parle anglais.*
May I help you?	*Est-ce que je peux vous aider?*
Yes, thank you.	*Oui, merci.*
What do you need?	*De quoi avez-vous besoin?*
I need some information.	*J'ai besoin de renseignements.*
I'm lost.	*Je suis perdu.*
Where is the hotel?	*Où est l'hôtel?*
Where are you going?	*Où allez-vous?*
I don't know.	*Je ne sais pas.*
I would like some coffee.	*Je voudrais du café.*
With pleasure.	*Avec plaisir.*

Lesson 1:8
Introducing Question Words

. . . .

Who?	*Qui?*
What?	*Qu'est-ce que?*
Where?	*Où?*
When?	*Quand?*
Why?	*Pourquoi?*
How?	*Comment?*
How much?; How many?	*Combien?*
Is there?; Are there?	*Y a-t-il?*

Useful Questions and Answers

. . . .

Who is that man?	*Qui est cet homme?*
He's the manager.	*C'est le gérant.*
Who are these people?	*Qui sont ces gens?*
They're students.	*Ce sont des étudiants.*
What are you doing? (Informal)	*Qu'est-ce que tu fais?*
I'm cooking.	*Je fais la cuisine.*
What do you want? (Formal)	*Qu'est-ce que vous voulez?*
I want to eat.	*Je veux manger.*
Where are you going? (Informal)	*Où vas-tu?*
I'm going to the museum.	*Je vais au musée.*
Where are the tickets?	*Où sont les billets?*
They're in the drawer.	*Ils sont dans le tiroir.*
Where is the Louvre located?	*Où se trouve le Louvre?*
In the first district.	*Dans le premier arrondissement.*
Where is the ATM?	*Où est le distributeur automatique?*
When do we leave?	*Quand partons-nous?*

We leave tomorrow morning.

Nous partons demain matin.

When is checkout time?

Quand faut-il régler la note?

How much does this bottle of wine cost?

Combien coûte cette bouteille de vin?

It costs 30 euros.

Elle coûte trente euros.

How many suitcases do you have?

Combien de valises avez-vous?

I have two suitcases.

J'ai deux valises.

You Can Count on Me: An Overview of Numbers

1	*un*
2	*deux*
3	*trois*
4	*quatre*
5	*cinq*
6	*six*
7	*sept*
8	*huit*
9	*neuf*
10	*dix*
11	*onze*
12	*douze*
13	*treize*
14	*quatorze*
15	*quinze*
16	*seize*
17	*dix-sept*
18	*dix-huit*
19	*dix-neuf*
20	*vingt*

With numbers 21 to 69, you combine the tens with the words for numbers 1 to 9.

21	*vingt et un*
22	*vingt-deux*
30	*trente*
31	*trente et un*
32	*trente-deux*
40	*quarante*
41	*quarante et un*
42	*quarante-deux*
50	*cinquante*
51	*cinquante et un*
52	*cinquante-deux*
60	*soixante*
61	*soixante et un*
62	*soixante-deux*

With the numbers 70 to 79, combine the tens with the tens.

70	*soixante-dix*
71	*soixante et onze*
72	*soixante-douze*

With the numbers 80 to 89, combine the number 4, the number 20, and the ones. For example, in French 80 is four 20s, 81 is four 20s plus 1, and so forth.

80	*quatre-vingts*
81	*quatre-vingt-un*
82	*quatre-vingt-deux*

For numbers 90 to 99, combine the number 4, the number 20, and the tens. For example, 90 is four 20s plus 10, 91 is four 20s plus 11, and so forth. (The *plus* isn't included in the expression.)

90	*quatre-vingt-dix*
91	*quatre-vingt-onze*
92	*quatre-vingt-douze*
100	*cent*
101	*cent un*
102	*cent deux*
150	*cent cinquante*
200	*deux cents*
500	*cinq cents*
1,000	*mille*

Lesson 1:11
Talking about Time

● ●

Time-related terms

time	*l'heure*
hour	*l'heure*
minute	*minute*
second	*seconde*
morning	*le matin*
afternoon	*l'après-midi*
evening	*le soir*
night	*la nuit*
day	*le jour*
today	*aujourd'hui*
yesterday	*hier*
tomorrow	*demain*

Time questions and answers

Do you have a minute?	*Avez-vous une minute?*
Do you have the time?	*Avez-vous l'heure?*
What time is it?	*Quelle heure est-il?*
It's late.	*Il est tard.*
It's early.	*Il est tôt.*
It's 8 in the morning.	*Il est huit heures du matin.*
It's noon.	*Il est midi.*

It's 5 in the afternoon.	*Il est cinq heures de l'après-midi.*
It's 7 in the evening.	*Il est sept heures du soir.*
It's a quarter past 7.	*Il est sept heures et quart.*
It's 7:30.	*Il est sept heures et demie.*
It's a quarter to 8.	*Il est huit heures moins le quart.*

Going through the Calendar and Forming Dates

*T*he days of the week and the months of the year aren't capitalized in French.

Days of the week

Monday	*lundi*
Tuesday	*mardi*
Wednesday	*mercredi*
Thursday	*jeudi*
Friday	*vendredi*
Saturday	*samedi*
Sunday	*dimanche*

When you're writing a date in French, you put the numbers in a different order than you would if you were writing it in English. You start with the day, then you write the month, and then the year. For example, to express September 27, 2006, you would write 27/9/06 instead of 9/27/06.

Months of the year

January	*janvier*
February	*février*
March	*mars*
April	*avril*
May	*mai*
June	*juin*
July	*juillet*
August	*août*
September	*septembre*
October	*octobre*
November	*novembre*
December	*décembre*

Common questions and answers

What day is it?	*Quel jour sommes-nous?*
It's Friday.	*C'est vendredi.*
What's the date?	*Quelle est la date?*
It's the first of May.	*C'est le premier mai.*
It's December 3.	*C'est le trois décembre.*
It's August 20.	*C'est le vingt août.*

 Only cardinal numbers are used for dates, except for the first of the month, which uses the ordinal number *premier* (first). For example, you say *c'est le premier janvier,* but you say *c'est le deux janvier.*

Directions

• •

east	*est*
west	*ouest*
north	*nord*
south	*sud*
to the right	*à droite*
to the left	*à gauche*
turn right	*tournez à droite*
turn left	*tournez à gauche*
straight ahead	*tout droit*
across	*en face de*
in front of	*devant*
in back of	*derrière*
next to	*à côté de*
between	*entre*
near; close	*près de*
far	*loin de*
street	*rue*
the next street	*la prochaine rue*
at the corner of	*au coin de*
downtown	*au centre-ville*
Can you tell me where that is?	*Pouvez-vous me dire où ça se trouve?*

Can you show me where that is?	*Pouvez-vous me montrer où ça se trouve?*
Are we near the theater?	*Est-ce que nous sommes près du théâtre?*
Here/there it is.	*Le/la voilà.*
You're far from the mall.	*Vous êtes loin du centre commercial.*

Welcome and Overview of CD2: The Nitty-Gritty: Language Structure

• •

*I*n the lessons on this CD, you discover how to use all the important parts of speech, including nouns, verbs, adjectives, pronouns, and more. Then you hear and practice simple sentences and questions.

Singular Nouns

School

college
student
teacher (elementary) (M/F)
teacher; professor
computer
desk
chair
book
notebook

École

université
étudiant
instituteur/institutrice
professeur
ordinateur
bureau
chaise
livre
cahier

Downtown

store
grocery store
supermarket
bakery
post office
movie theater
restaurant

Centre-ville

magasin
épicerie
supermarché
boulangerie
poste
cinéma
restaurant

hospital	*hôpital*
drugstore	*pharmacie*
hotel	*hôtel*
church	*église*

Occupations

Métiers

doctor	*médecin*
nurse (M/F)	*infirmier/infirmière*
lawyer (M/F)	*avocat/avocate*
police officer	*agent de police*
firefighter	*pompier*
accountant	*comptable*
banker	*banquier*
architect	*architecte*
engineer	*ingénieur*

Lesson 2:3
Plural Nouns

• •

*I*n order to make a noun plural, most often you add an *-s* to the end. However, you don't add anything if the noun already ends in an *-s*, *-x*, or *-z*. Add an *-x* to nouns that end in *-eau*, *-eu*, or *-ou* to make them plural.

 Final consonants aren't pronounced in French, so you don't have to worry about a difference in pronunciation between the singular and plural forms of nouns. Only in some cases can you hear the difference, such as with nouns that have a completely different form in the plural, like *l'oeil* (the eye) and *les yeux* (the eyes), and nouns that end in *-al* and change to *-aux* in the plural, like *animal* (animal) and *animaux* (animals).

professors	*professeurs*
books	*livres*
classmates	*camarades de classe*
computers	*ordinateurs*
stores	*magasins*
doctors	*médecins*
policemen	*agents de police*
shopkeepers	*commerçants*
offices	*bureaux*
hospitals	*hôpitaux*

 Hôpitaux (hospitals) is the only noun from the list of nouns in Lesson 2:2 in which the pronunciation of the plural is different from the singular.

Articles

* *

*T*he indefinite articles in French are *un* and *une*. You use *un* in front of masculine singular nouns and *une* in front of feminine singular nouns. The indefinite article for plural nouns is *des*. The definite articles in French are *le* for masculine nouns and *la* for feminine nouns. The definite article for plural nouns is *les*.

A/An

a building	*un bâtiment*
an airplane	*un avion*
a question	*une question*
a sentence	*une phrase*
a house	*une maison*

The

the office	*le bureau*
the train	*le train*
the passport	*le passeport*
the family	*la famille*
the bill	*la facture*
the play	*la pièce*
the map	*la carte*

Lesson 2:5
Demonstrative Pronouns

● ●

Depending on the context of the sentence, the same demonstrative adjectives can mean "this" or "that" in the singular and "these" and "those" in the plural. However, in order to emphasize the difference, you can add the suffix *-ci* (this; these) and *-là* (that; those) to the noun. For example, consider *ce livre-ci* (this book), *ce livre-là* (that book), *ces livres-ci* (these books), and *ces livres-là* (those books).

You use *ce* to indicate masculine singular nouns, *cette* with feminine singular nouns, *cet* with masculine singular nouns that begin with a vowel or a mute *h*, and *ces* with both masculine and feminine plural nouns.

This/That	*Ce/Cet (-te)*
this morning	*ce matin*
this water	*cette eau*
this woman	*cette femme*
this man	*cet homme*
this hotel	*cet hôtel*

These/Those	*Ces*
these people	*ces gens*
these students	*ces étudiants*
these children	*ces enfants*

Adjectives

* *

*I*n French, an adjective agrees in gender (masculine or feminine) and in number (singular or plural) with the noun it modifies.

Aside from some minor exceptions, set rules apply to the transformation of the adjective from the masculine to the feminine:

> ✔ If the adjective already ends in an unaccentuated *-e,* it doesn't change in the feminine.
>
> ✔ If the adjective ends in an accentuated *-e* (or *é*), you add *-e* to make it feminine.
>
> ✔ If an adjective ends in a consonant, you add *-e* to make it feminine.
>
> ✔ If an adjective ends in *-x,* you replace the *-x* with *-se.*
>
> ✔ If an adjective ends in *-f,* you replace the *-f* with *-ve.*

Just like with nouns, you add *-s* to make adjectives plural. If the adjective already ends in *-s, -z,* or *-x,* leave it alone. Making the adjectives plural, however, doesn't change their pronunciations.

Note: In the following list, the French terms are presented in the following format: Masculine (plural)/Feminine (plural).

Colors

yellow	*jaune(s)*
pink	*rose(s)*
red	*rouge(s)*
orange	*orange*
green	*vert(s)/verte(s)*
white	*blanc(s)/blanche(s)*
black	*noir(s)/noire(s)*
blue	*bleu(s)/bleue(s)*

Common adjectives

big	*grand(s)/grande(s)*
small	*petit(s)/petite(s)*
fast	*rapide(s)*
slow	*lent(s)/lente(s)*
easy	*facile(s)*
difficult	*difficile(s)*
happy	*heureux/heureuse(s)*
sad	*triste(s)*
handsome; pretty	*beau(x)/belle(s)*
hot	*chaud(s)/chaude(s)*
cold	*froid(s)/froide(s)*
young	*jeune(s)*
old	*vieux/vieille(s)*
new	*nouveau(x)/nouvelle(s)*

Degrees of Adjectives

bigger	*plus grand*
biggest	*le plus grand*
smaller	*plus petit*
smallest	*le plus petit*
faster	*plus rapide*
fastest	*le plus rapide*

For example:

My car is older than your car.	*Ma voiture est plus vieille que ta voiture.*
It's the coldest day of the year.	*C'est le jour le plus froid de l'année.*
An airplane is faster than a train.	*Un avion est plus rapide qu'un train.*

To Be or Not to Be: A Very Important Verb

. . . .

To be	*Être*
I am	*Je suis*
you are (S)	*tu es*
he/it is (M)	*il est*
she/it is (F)	*elle est*
we are	*nous sommes*
you are (P/Formal)	*vous êtes*
they are (M)	*ils sont*
they are (F)	*elles sont*
They are young.	*Ils sont jeunes.*
We are late.	*Nous sommes en retard.*
I am optimistic.	*Je suis optimiste.*

Verbs

* *

to go	*aller*
to come	*venir*
to wait	*attendre*
to speak	*parler*
to write	*écrire*
to walk	*marcher*
to run	*courir*
to eat	*manger*
to drink	*boire*
to work	*travailler*
to study	*étudier*
to call	*appeler*
to ask	*demander*
to look	*regarder*
to think	*penser*
to try	*essayer*
to see	*voir*

| to hear | *entendre* |
| to listen | *écouter* |

There are three categories of regular verbs in French: Those whose infinitives end in *-er, -ir,* or *-re*.

-er Verbs

For *-er* verbs, drop the *-er* of the infinitive and add the following endings: *-e, -es, -e, -ons, -ez, -ent*.

to speak	*parler*
I speak	*Je parle*
you speak (S/Informal)	*tu parles*
he/she speaks	*il/elle parle*
we speak	*nous parlons*
you speak (P/Formal)	*vous parlez*
they speak (M/F)	*ils/elles parlent*

-ir Verbs

For *-ir* verbs, drop the *-r* of the infinitive and add the following endings: *-s, -s, -t, -ssons, -ssez, -ssent*.

to finish	*finir*
I finish	*Je finis*
you finish (S/Informal)	*tu finis*
he/she finishes	*il/elle finit*
we finish	*nous finissons*

| you finish (P/Formal) | *vous finissez* |
| they finish (M/F) | *ils/elles finissent* |

-re Verbs

For -re verbs, drop the -re of the infinitive and add the following endings: -s, -s, (nothing), -ons, -ez, -ent.

to wait	*attendre*
I wait	*J'attends*
you wait (S/Informal)	*tu attends*
he/she waits	*il/elle attend*
we wait	*nous attendons*
you wait (P/Formal)	*vous attendez*
they wait (M/F)	*ils/elles attendent*

Common irregular verbs

There are some irregular verbs that have different conjugations. Below are two of the most important of these types of verbs: *avoir* (to have) and *aller* (to go).

to have	*avoir*
I have	*J'ai*
you have (S/Informal)	*tu as*
he/she has	*il/elle a*
we have	*nous avons*
you have (P/Formal)	*vous avez*
they have (M/F)	*ils/elles ont*

to go	*aller*
I go	*Je vais*
you go (S/Informal)	*tu vas*
he/she goes	*il/elle va*
we go	*nous allons*
you go (P/Formal)	*vous allez*
they go (M/F)	*ils/elles vont*

Verbs and Tenses

* *

The past tense

The *passé composé* is used to indicate a completed action in the past. As the name indicates, the *passé composé* is composed of two parts: an auxiliary and a past participle. The two auxiliary verbs are *avoir* and *être,* with *avoir* used in most situations. To use these auxiliary verbs, add the past participle of the verb of your choice. The past tense is formed as follows:

to speak	*parler*
I spoke	*J'ai parlé*
you spoke (S/Informal)	*tu as parlé*
he/she spoke	*il/elle a parlé*
we spoke	*nous avons parlé*
you spoke (P/Formal)	*vous avez parlé*
they spoke (M/F)	*ils/elles ont parlé*
to wait	*attendre*
I waited	*J'ai attendu*
you waited (S/Informal)	*tu as attendu*
he/she waited	*il/elle a attendu*
we waited	*nous avons attendu*
you waited (P/Formal)	*vous avez attendu*
they waited (M/F)	*ils/elles ont attendu*

The future tense using aller

The immediate future, or the near future, as it's sometimes called, is formed by conjugating the verb *aller* (to go) in the present tense and adding the infinitive of any verb of your choice. For example:

I am going to read.	*Je vais lire.*
They are going to skate.	*Ils vont patiner.*
We are going to leave.	*Nous allons partir.*

Present, past, and future examples

You eat shrimp.	*Tu manges des crevettes.*
You ate shrimp.	*Tu as mangé des crevettes.*
You are going to eat shrimp.	*Tu vas manger des crevettes.*
He reads the newspaper.	*Il lit le journal.*
He read the newspaper.	*Il a lu le journal.*
He is going to read the newspaper.	*Il va lire le journal.*
We speak French.	*Nous parlons français.*
We spoke French.	*Nous avons parlé français.*
We are going to speak French.	*Nous allons parler français.*

Negatives

• •

*T*he negative in French is composed of two parts: *ne* and *pas*. Place *ne* in front of the conjugated verb and *pas* after the conjugated verb.

I'm not waiting.	*Je n'attends pas.*
You don't understand. (S/Informal)	*Tu ne comprends pas.*
He isn't working.	*Il ne travaille pas.*
She can't swim.	*Elle ne peut pas nager.*
We don't like milk.	*Nous n'aimons pas le lait.*

If the verb begins with a vowel or a mute *h*, then drop the *-e* of *ne* and add an apostrophe to make it *n'*.

Prepositions

• •

Common prepositions

on	*sur*
above	*au-dessus*
in	*dans*
inside	*dedans*
outside	*dehors*
under	*sous*
underneath	*au-dessous*
in front of	*devant*
in back of; behind	*derrière*
next to	*à côté de*
across	*en face de*
near	*près de*
far	*loin de*
in the middle of	*au milieu de*
around	*autour de*
between	*entre*
among	*parmi*
of; from	*de*

Example phrases

on the table	*sur la table*
above the refrigerator	*au-dessus du frigo*
in the cabinet	*dans le placard*
inside the house	*dans la maison*
outside the school	*en dehors de l'école*
under the table	*sous la table*
behind the bed	*derrière le lit*
near the airport	*près de l'aéroport*

Conjunctions

• •

and	*et*
but	*mais*
or	*ou*
neither	*ni*
either	*soit*
yet	*pourtant*
so	*ainsi*
therefore	*donc*
because	*parce que*
if	*si*
although	*bien que*
unless	*à moins que*

Example sentences

I have a son and a daughter.	*J'ai un fils et une fille.*
I like shrimp, but it makes me sick.	*J'aime les crevettes mais elles me rendent malade.*

Forming Simple Sentences

● ●

What's the weather like?	*Quel temps fait-il?*
It's hot.	*Il fait chaud.*
I'm going home.	*Je rentre.*
You look pretty.	*Tu as l'air joli(e).*
The restroom is on your right.	*Les toilettes sont à votre droite.*
Those seats are taken.	*Ces places-là sont prises.*
Those boys are cousins.	*Ces garçons-là sont cousins.*

Introducing More Complete Sentences

We are going to shop for two hours and then go to a movie.

Nous allons faire les courses pendant deux heures et puis nous allons au cinéma.

We are going to eat dinner (to dine) at 7.

Nous allons dîner à sept heures.

I would like to buy this sweater.

Je voudrais acheter ce pull.

Forming Questions

* *

What time does the restaurant close?	*À quelle heure le restaurant ferme?*
Where does your daughter live? (Informal)	*Où habite ta fille?*
When is the meeting?	*Quand est la réunion?*
How do I get to the office?	*Comment est-ce que je vais au bureau?*

Welcome and Overview of CD3: Real-World Situations

*I*n these lessons, you discover vocabulary for making conversation in the workplace. You also practice interacting with native speakers, and you begin forming sentences and phrases when asking for help or directions, eating out, staying at a hotel, banking, and shopping.

At the Office

. . . .

Office equipment and supplies

pen	*un stylo*
pencil	*un crayon*
desk	*un bureau*
chair	*une chaise*
computer	*un ordinateur*
screen	*un écran*
keyboard	*un clavier*
mouse	*une souris*
USB key	*une clef USB*
notebook	*un carnet*
Web site	*un site Internet*
e-mail	*un courrier électronique*

Meetings

interview	*un entretien*
deadline	*une échéance*
agenda	*l'ordre du jour*
minutes	*un compte-rendu*
appointment book	*un agenda*
appointment	*un rendez-vous*

Business departments

sales	*ventes*
marketing	*marketing*
finance	*finance*
accounting	*comptabilité*
human resources	*ressources humaines*
legal	*département juridique*
research and development	*recherche et développement*
technical support	*support technique*

Colleagues

assistant; secretary	*secrétaire*
chief executive officer	*président directeur général (PDG)*
chief financial officer	*directeur financier*
manager (M/F)	*directeur/directrice*
supervisor (M/F)	*surveillant/surveillante*
coordinator (M/F)	*coordinateur/coordinatrice*

Verbs

to set up an appointment	*prendre un rendez-vous*
to cancel an appointment	*annuler un rendez-vous*
to discuss	*discuter*
to identify	*identifier*

to solve	*résoudre*
to reconcile	*réconcilier*
to fix	*réparer*

Example sentences

We're going to have a conference call at 2:00.	*Nous allons avoir une conférence par téléphone à quatorze heures.*
May I borrow a pen and a notepad?	*Puis-je emprunter un stylo et un bloc-notes?*
The printer isn't working.	*L'imprimante ne fonctionne pas.*
Send me an e-mail. (Formal)	*Envoyez-moi un courrier électronique.*

On the Job

* *

Professions

police officer	*un policier*
nurse (M/F)	*un infirmier/une infirmière*
doctor	*un médecin*
lawyer (M/F)	*un avocat/une avocate*
teacher (M/F)	*un instituteur/une institutrice*
artist	*un artiste*
journalist	*un journaliste*
cook (M/F)	*un cuisinier/une cuisinière*
hostess	*une hôtesse*
server (M/F)	*un serveur/une serveuse*
firefighter	*un pompier*
carpenter	*un charpentier*
electrician	*un électricien*
plumber	*un plombier*
gardener	*un jardinier*
driver	*un chauffeur*

Verbs

to help	*aider*
to build	*construire*
to clean	*nettoyer*
to drive	*conduire*
to place	*placer*

Making Small Talk

* *

My name is . . .	*Je m'appelle . . .*
I am from . . .	*Je suis de . . .*
Where are you from? (Formal)	*D'où venez-vous?*
What is your profession? (Formal)	*Quel est votre métier?*
How old are you? (Formal)	*Quel âge avez-vous?*
Where do you live? (Formal)	*Où habitez-vous?*
What do you like to do for fun? (Informal)	*Qu'est-ce que tu aimes faire pour t'amuser?*
What do you play? (Informal)	*À quoi joues-tu?*
I play golf.	*Je joue au golf.*
I play soccer.	*Je joue au football.*
I play football.	*Je joue au football américain.*
I play tennis.	*Je joue au tennis.*
I'm a big sports fan.	*Je suis un grand supporter de sport.*
I'm a student. (M/F)	*Je suis étudiant/étudiante.*
How many children do you have?	*Combien d'enfants avez-vous?*
I have three children.	*J'ai trois enfants.*

Making Appointments

- -

We should have coffee tomorrow morning.

On devrait prendre un café demain matin.

Do you want to go to the movies? (Informal)

Tu veux aller au cinéma?

I'm available this afternoon. Do you want to go to the movies? (P)

Je suis disponible cet après-midi. Voulez-vous aller au cinéma?

I'm not free on Friday, so how about Sunday?

Je ne suis pas libre vendredi, alors si on y allait dimanche?

Can we schedule the meeting for 10:00 Wednesday morning?

Pouvons-nous prévoir la réunion pour dix heures mercredi matin?

We should all go to the park tomorrow.

Nous devrions tous aller au parc demain.

We should have dinner together on Saturday night.

On devrait dîner ensemble samedi soir.

Why don't we meet in the town center?

Nous devrions-nous retrouver au centre-ville?

Making Travel Arrangements

* *

Vocabulary

ticket	*un billet*
reservation	*une réservation*
flight	*un vol*
suitcase	*une valise*
backpack	*un sac à dos*
bag	*un sac*
baggage	*des bagages*
train	*un train*

Verbs

to reserve	*réserver*
to cancel	*annuler*
to arrive	*arriver*
to leave	*partir*
to pick up someone (from the airport, for example)	*chercher quelqu'un*

Example phrases

I would like to reserve a ticket.	*Je voudrais réserver un billet.*
I would like to take the 7:00 flight.	*J'aimerais prendre le vol de sept heures.*
I would like to purchase two tickets to New York.	*Je voudrais acheter deux billets pour New York.*
We have three suitcases and two handbags.	*Nous avons trois valises et deux sacs à main.*
Can I take this bag as a carry-on?	*Est-ce que je peux prendre ce sac en cabine avec moi?*
Do you have any discounts for students?	*Avez-vous un rabais pour étudiants?*
What time should I arrive?	*A quelle heure faut-il arriver?*
How far is the hotel from the train station?	*Est-ce que l'hôtel est loin de la gare?*
Which hotel is cheaper?	*Quel hôtel est moins cher?*
Which hotel is the cheapest?	*Quel est l'hôtel le moins cher?*
How much does the ticket cost?	*Combien coûte le billet?*

Asking for Directions

* *

Vocabulary

map	*une carte*
district	*un quartier*
town	*une ville*
city	*une ville*
downtown	*le centre-ville*
street	*une rue*
corner	*un coin*
direction	*une direction*
right	*à droite de*
left	*à gauche de*
straight	*tout droit*
around	*autour de*
next to	*à côté de*
between	*entre*
close	*près de*
far	*loin de*
center	*centre*

Example phrases

May I ask you for directions?	*Est-ce que je peux vous demander mon chemin?*
Where is the hotel?	*Où est l'hôtel?*
The hotel is next to the train station.	*L'hôtel est à côté de la gare.*
What street is the movie theater on?	*Dans quelle rue se trouve le cinéma?*
The movie theater is on your right.	*Le cinéma est à votre droite.*
Is the school far from here?	*Est-ce que l'école est loin d'ici?*
How do I get to the museum?	*Comment est-ce que je vais au musée?*
The museum is about 1 kilometer and a half from here.	*Le musée est à peu près un kilomètre et demi d'ici.*
Turn right, and it's the first street on your left.	*Tournez à droite et c'est la première rue à votre gauche.*
Where is the nearest bank?	*Où est la banque la plus proche?*
The school is in the center of town.	*L'école est au centre de la ville.*
Go straight and you'll find it.	*Allez tout droit et vous le trouverez.*

Asking for and Getting Help

* *

Vocabulary

Help!	*Au secours!*
health	*la santé*
hospital	*l'hôpital*
doctor	*le médecin*
pharmacy	*la pharmacie*
aspirin	*l'aspirine*
medication	*des médicaments*
headache	*un mal de tête*
stomachache	*un mal de ventre*
injury	*une blessure*
pain	*une douleur*
infection	*une infection*

Example phrases

Will you help me?	*Est-ce que vous pourrez m'aider?*
Please help me!	*Aidez-moi s'il vous plaît!*
She fell down the stairs and needs a doctor.	*Elle est tombée dans l'escalier et elle a besoin d'un médecin.*

We're lost and can't find the hotel.

Nous sommes perdus et ne pouvons pas trouver l'hôtel.

He's feeling sick and has a fever. Where is the hospital?

Il se sent malade et il a de la fièvre. Où est l'hôpital?

I've just been robbed.

On vient de me voler.

We need to speak to a police officer.

Nous avons besoin de parler à un agent de police.

Where is the consulate?

Où est le consulat?

At the Restaurant

* *

I would like some water.	*Je voudrais de l'eau.*
Do you serve orange juice?	*Servez-vous du jus d'orange?*
What kind of vegetables do you have?	*Quelle sorte de légumes avez-vous?*
What kind of fish is on the menu?	*Quelle sorte de poissons avez-vous au menu?*
What is today's special?	*Quel est le plat du jour?*
I'd like some bread.	*Je voudrais du pain.*

Lesson 3:10
At the Hotel

● ●

What rooms do you have available?

Quelles chambres avez-vous de disponible?

I'd like a double room.

Je voudrais une chambre pour deux.

Does the room have air conditioning?

Est-ce que la chambre a la climatisation?

I'd like to have a twin-size bed.

Je voudrais avoir un lit à une place.

You need to check out by 12:00.

Vous devez régler la note avant midi.

We want to cancel our reservation.

Nous voulons annuler notre réservation.

Room service, please.

Service en chambre, s'il vous plaît.

At the Bank

. . . .

What is the exchange rate today?	*Quel est le taux de change aujourd'hui?*
Today's exchange rate is 1 euro for $1.23	*Le taux de change du jour est un euro pour un dollar vingt-trois.*
I would like to exchange $100.	*Je voudrais échanger cent dollars.*
How do I open a checking account?	*Comment ouvre-t-on un compte courant?*
Do you have any branches in Italy?	*Avez-vous des agences en Italie?*
I would like to buy traveler's checks.	*Je voudrais acheter des chèques de voyage.*
I would like to make change for this bill.	*Je voudrais de la monnaie en échange de ce billet.*

At the Store

- -

Verbs

to buy	*acheter*
to pay	*payer*
to decide	*décider*
to try on	*essayer*
to look	*regarder*

Example phrases

I like that one.	*J'aime celui-là.*
I would like to purchase these shoes.	*Je voudrais acheter ces chaussures.*
How much is this shirt?	*Combien coûte cette chemise?*
I'm looking for a red skirt.	*Je cherche une jupe rouge.*
Are these pants on sale?	*Est-ce que ce pantalon est en solde?*
May I return this item?	*Puis-je retourner cet article?*
Can I pay cash or credit?	*Puis-je payer comptant ou par carte de crédit?*
No thank you, I'm just looking.	*Merci, je ne fais que regarder.*

These watches are expensive.   *Ces montres sont chères.*

He can't decide what to buy.   *Il n'arrive pas à se décider*
                                       à ce qu'il va acheter.

Shopping for groceries

I have to go grocery
shopping.   *Je dois faire les provisions.*

We need milk, eggs,   *Il nous faut du lait, des*
and bread.   *oeufs, et du pain.*

Let's pay at the cash   *Payons à la caisse.*
register.

Mini-Dictionaries

French-English Mini-Dictionary

à bientôt (ah byan-to): see you soon

à côté de (ah ko-tay duh): next to

à demain (ah duh-man): see you tomorrow

à droite (ah drwaht): on the right

à gauche (ah gosh): on the left

à l'heure (ah luh): on time

absolument (ahb-so-lew-mahN): absolutely

accepter (ah-ksehp-tay): to accept

acheter (ah-shuh-tay): to buy

addition (ah-dee-syohn) f: check

adresse (ah-drehss) f: address

adresse électronique (ah-dreh-say-lehk-tro-neek) f: e-mail address

affaires (ah-fehr) f: business

aider (eh-day): to help

aimer (ay-may): to like; to love

aller (ah-lay): to go

aller-retour (ah-lay ruh-toor) m: round trip

aller-simple (ah-lay sahnpl) m: one-way (ticket)

ami (ah-mee) m: friend

amie (ah-mee) f: friend

appeler (ah-pehl-lay): to call

argent (ahr-zhahn) m: money

arrêt (ah-reh) m: stop

arriver (ah-ree-vay): to arrive

assiette (ah-syeht) f: plate

attendre (ah-tehn-druh): to wait

au fond (o fohN): in the back

au revoir (ohr-vwahr): good bye

aujourd'hui (o-zhoor-dwee): today

aussi (o-see): also

avocat (ah-vo-kah) m: lawyer

avoir (ah-vwahr): to have

banane (ba-naN) f: banana

basket (bahs-keht) m: basketball

baskets (bahs-keht) f: sneakers

beau (bo): nice; beautiful

bicyclette (bee-see-kleht) f: bicycle

bien sûr (byan sewr): of course

bière (byehr) f: beer

billet (bee-yeh) m: ticket

bizarre (beez-ahr): weird; bizarre

blanc (blahn): white

bleu (bluh) m: blue

boeuf (buhf) m: beef

boire (bwar): to drink

bon (bohN): good

bonjour (bohN-zhoor): good day

bonne nuit (bohN ne-wee): good night

bonsoir (bohn-swahr): good night

bottes (boht) f: boots

boucherie (boo-shree) f: butcher shop

boulangerie (boo-lahn-zhree) f: bakery

bras (brah) m: arm

bruyant (bree-ahn): noisy

bureau (bew-ro) m: office

ça va (sah vah): okay

café (kah-fay) m: coffee

caisse (kehs) f: the cash register

campagne (cahN-pahn-yuh) f: countryside

carte de crédit (kahr-tuh duh cray-dee) f: credit card

celle-ci (sehl-see) f: this one

celle-là (sehl-lah) f: that one

celui-ci (suh-lwee-see) m: this one

celui-là (suh-lwee-lah) m: that one

chapeau (shap-oh) m: hat

chaud (sho): warm; hot

chemise (ewn shuh-meez) f: shirt

chemisier (shuh-mee-zyay) m: blouse

cher (shehr): expensive

choisir (shwah-zeer): to choose

clair (klehr): light-colored

code postal (cohd pohs-tahl) m: zip code

coffre (kohfr) m: trunk

collègue (koh-lehg) m: co-worker

comment (koh-mahN): how

compagnie (kohn-pah-nyee) f: company

conduire (kohn-dweer): to drive

costume de bains (kohs-tewm duh ban) m: bathing suit

cou (koo) m: neck

couleur (koo-luhr) f: color

couteau (koo-to) m: knife

cravate (krah-vaht) f: tie

crudités (krew-dee-tay) f: raw vegetables

cuillère (kwee-yehr) f: spoon; teaspoon

d'accord (dah-kohr): all right; okay

danser (dahn-say): to dance

dehors (duh-ohr): outside

déjeuner (day-zhuh-nay) m: to lunch

dentiste (dahN-teest) m: dentist

dessert (deh-sehr) m: dessert

deux (duh): two

devoir (duh-vwahr): to have to

docteur (dohk-tuhr) m: doctor

doigt (dwah) m: finger

donner (do-nay): to give

dormir (dor-meer): to sleep

eau (lo) f: water

échecs (ayshehk) m/pl: chess

elle (ehl) f: she

elles (ehl) f: they

employé (ahN-plwa-yay) m: employee

en retard (ahn ruh-tahr): late

enchanté (ahN-shahN-tay): delighted

enfant (ahN-fahN) m/f: child

ennuyeux (ehn-wee-uh): boring

entrées (ahn-tray) f: appetizers

épaule (ay-pohl) f: shoulder

épicerie (ay-pees-ree) f: grocery store; general store

être (ehtr): to be

étroit (ay-trwah): narrow

facile (fah-seel): easy

faim (faN): hungry

fatigué (fah-tee-gay): tired

femme (fahm) f: wife

fenêtre (fuh-nehtr) f: window

fêtes (feht) f: holidays

figure (fee-gewr) f: face

fille (fee-y) f: daughter; girl

fils (fees) m: son

fin (fahN) f: end

finir (fee-neer): to finish

fleur (fluhr) f: flower

foncé (fohN-say): dark

football (fewt-bahl) m: soccer

football Américain (fewt-bahl ah-may-ree-kehn) m: American football

fourchette (ewn foor-sheht) f: fork

fraise (frehz) f: strawberry

frère (frerh) m: brother

froid (frwah): cold

fromage (fro-mazh) m: cheese

fruits (lay frwee) m: fruit

gagner (gahn-yay): to win

garçon (gahr-sohN) m: boy

gare (gah) f: train station

glace (glahs) f: ice cream

grand (grahNd): big; tall; large

grand magasin (grahN mah-gah-zanN) m: department store

grippe (greep) f: flu

guitare (gee-tahr) f: guitar

habiter (ah-bee-tay): to live

il (eel) m: he

il y a (ee-lee-yah): there is

ils (eel) m: they

imperméable (an-pehr-may-ahbl) m: raincoat

infirmier (aN-feer-myay) m: nurse

ingénieur (aN-zhay-nyuhr) m: engineer

jardin (zhahr-daN) m: yard

jaune (zhon): yellow

je (zhuh): I

jean (dzheen) m: jeans

joli (zho-lee): pretty

jouer (zhoo-ay): to play

jour (zhoor) m: day

jupe (zhewp) f: skirt

jusqu'à (zhews-kah): until

là-bas (lah-bah): over there

laine (lehn) f: wool

large (lahrzh): large

légumes (lay-gewm)
m: vegetables

lendemain (lahN-duh-mahN)
m: next day

livre (leevr) f: pound
(weight)

lui (lew-ee) m: him

madame (mah-dahm)
f: madam; missus

magasin (mah-gah-zan)
m: store

main (mahn) f: hand

maintenant (man-tuh-
nahN): now

mais (meh): but

maison (meh-zohN) f: house

maladie (mah-lah-dee)
f: illness

manger (mahn-zhay): to eat

manquer (mahn-kay):
to miss

manteau (mahN-to) m: coat

marchand (mahr-shan)
m: vendor

mari (mah-ree) m: husband

marron (mah-rohN): brown

mauvais (mo-veh): bad

médecin (mayd-saN)
m: physician

même (mehm): even

mer (mehr) f: ocean

merci (mehr-see): thank you

mère (mehr) f: mother

mettre (meh-truh): to put

moderne (moh-dehrn):
modern

moi (mwa): me

monsieur (muh-syuh)
m: mister

montagne (mohn-tahn-yuh)
f: mountain

montre (mohntr) f: watch

montrer (mohN-tray):
to show

natation (nah-tah-see-ohN)
f: swimming

neige (nehzh) m: snow

nez (nay) m: nose

noir (nwahr) m: black

nom (nohN) m: last name

nous (noo): we

numéro de téléphone
(new-may-ro duh tay-lay-
fohn) m: phone number

œil (uhy) m: eye

orange (or-ahnzh) f: orange

oreille (oh-rehy) f: ear

où (oo): where

pain (pan) m: bread

pantalon (pahN-tah-lohN) m: slacks

parfait (pahr-feh): perfect

parler (pahr-lay): to speak; to talk

partir (pahr-teer): to leave

pas du tout (pah dew too): not at all

passeport (pahs-pohr) m: passport

pâtisserie (pah-tees-ree) f: pastry shop

pays (peh-ee) m: country

penser (pahN-say): to think

père (pehr) m: father

personnes (pehr-sohn) f/pl: people

petit (puh-teet): small; short

petit déjeuner (puh-tee day-zhuh-nay) m: breakfast

petit-fils (puh-tee fees) m: grandson

petite-fille (puh-teet feey) f: granddaughter

petits pois (puh-tee pwa) m: peas

petits-enfants (puh-tee zahN-fahN) m/pl: grandchildren

photo (foh-toh) f: picture

piano (pee-ahn-oh) m: piano

pied (pyeh) m: foot

plage (plahzh) f: beach

pointure (pwan-tewr) f: shoe size

poisson (pwa-sohn) m: fish

poitrine (pwah-treen) f: chest

poivre (pwavr) m: pepper

police (poh-lees) f: police

pomme (pohm) f: apple

pommes de terre (pohm duh tehr) f: potatoes

porc (pohr) m: pork

porte (pohrt) f: door

porte-monnaie (pohrt-moh-neh) m: wallet

porter (pohr-tay): to wear

poulet (poo-leh) m: chicken

pourboire (poor-bwar) m: tip

pourquoi (poor-kwa): why

pouvoir (poo-vwar): can; may; to be able to

préférer (pray-fay-ray): to prefer

prendre (prahndr): to take

prénom (pray-nohN) m: first name

présenter (pray-zahN-tay): to introduce

professeur (pro-feh-suhr) m: high school teacher; college professor

puis (pew-ee): then

pull (pewl) m: sweater

qu'est-ce que (kehs-kuh): what

quand (kahN): when

quelle (kehl): which

quelque chose (kehl-kuh shoz): something

qui (kee): who

regarder (reh-gahr-day): to watch

rendre (rahndr): to return (something)

repas (ruh-pah) m: meal

répondre (ray-pohN-druh): to answer

rester (rehs-tay): to stay

retraité (ruh-treh-tay) m/f: retired person

robe (rohb) f: dress

rouge (roozh): red

rue (rew) f: street

sac (sahk) m: bag

salut (sah-lew): hi

secrétaire (suh-cray-tehr) m: secretary

séjour (say-zhoor) m: stay

sel (sehl) m: salt

semaine (suh-mehn) f: week

serveur (sehr-vuhr) m: waiter

serviette (sehr-vyeht) f: napkin

seulement (suhl-mahN): only

siège (syehzh) m: seat

slip (sleep) m: underpants

soeur (suhr) f: sister

soccer (soh-kehr) m: soccer (Canada)

soif (swaf): thirsty

soleil (soh-lehy) m: sun

sortir (sor-teer): to exit

soucoupe (soo-koop) f: saucer

sucre (sewkr) m: sugar

supermarché (sew-pehr-mahr-shay) m: supermarket

sur (sewr): on; on top of

sweat (sweet) m: sweatshirt

tant pis (tahN pee): too bad

tasse (tahs) f: cup

téléphoner (tay-lay-foh-nay): to telephone; to call

thé (tay) m: tea

toi (twa): you

tomate (to-maht) f: tomato

toujours (too-zhoor): always

tous (toos): all

train (trahn) m: train

travailler (trah-va-yay): to work

trop (tro): too much

tu (tew): you (informal)

un (uhN): one

valise (vah-leez) f: suitcase

veau (vo) m: veal

vendre (vahndr): to sell

venir (vuh-neer): to come

verre (vehr) m: glass

vert (vehr): green

veste (vehst) f: jacket

veston (vehs-tohN) m: man's suit jacket

viande (vyahnd) f: meat

ville (veel) f: city; town

vin (van) m: wine

voir (vwahr): to see

voiture (vwah-tewr) f: car

vol (vohl) m: flight

vouloir (voo-lwahr): to want

vous (voo): you (formal)

voyager (vwah-yazhay): to travel

English-French Mini-Dictionary

absolutely: **absolument**
(ahb-so-lew-mahN)

accept: **accepter**
(ah-ksehp-tay)

address: **adresse**
(ah-drehss) f

all: **tous** (toos)

all right; okay: **d'accord**
(dah-kohr)

also: **aussi** (o-see)

always: **toujours** (too-zhoor)

American football: **football
américain** (fewt-bahl ah-
may-ree-kehn) m

answer: **répondre**
(ray-pohN-druh)

appetizers: **entrées**
(ahn-tray) f

apple: **pomme** (pohm) f

arm: **bras** (brah) m

arrive: **arriver** (ah-ree-vay)

bad: **mauvais** (mo-veh)

bag: **sac** (sahk) m

bakery: **boulangerie**
(boo-lahn-zhree) f

banana: **banane** (ba-naN) f

basketball: **basket**
(bahs-keht) m

bathing suit: **costume de
bains** (kohs-tewm duh
ban) m

be: **être** (ehtr)

be able to: **pouvoir**
(poov-wahr)

beach: **plage** (plahzh) f

beef: **boeuf** (buhf) m

beer: **bière** (byehr) f

bicycle: **bicyclette**
(bee-see-kleht) f

big; tall; large: **grand**
(grahNd)

black: **noir** (nwahr)

blouse: **chemisier**
(shuh-mee-zyay) m

blue: **bleu** (bluh) m

boots: **bottes** (boht) f

boring: **ennuyeux**
(ehn-wee-uh)

boy: **garçon** (gahr-sohN) m

bread: **pain** (pan) m

breakfast: **petit déjeuner**
(puh-tee day-zhuh-nay) m

brother: **frère** (frerh) m

brown: **marron** (mah-rohN)

business: **affaires**
(ah-fehr) f

but: **mais** (meh)

butcher shop: **boucherie** (boo-shree) f

buy: **acheter** (ah-shuh-tay)

call: **appeler** (ah-pehl-lay)

can; may: **pouvoir** (poo-vwar)

car: **voiture** (vwah-tewr) f

cash register: **caisse** (kehs) f

check: **addition** (ah-dee-syohn) f

cheese: **fromage** (fro-mazh) m

chess: **échecs** (ayshehk) m/pl

chest: **poitrine** (pwah-treen) f

chicken: **poulet** (poo-leh) m

child: **enfant** (ahN-fahN) m/f

choose: **choisir** (shwah-zeer)

city: **ville** (veel) f

coat: **manteau** (mahN-to) m

coffee: **café** (kah-fay) m

cold: **froid** (frwah)

color: **couleur** (koo-luhr) f

come: **venir** (vuh-neer)

company: **compagnie** (kohn-pah-nyee) f

confectioner's shop: **pâtis-serie** (pah-tees-ree) f

country: **pays** (peh-ee) m

countryside: **campagne** (cahN-pahn-yuh) f

co-worker: **collègue** (koh-lehg) m

credit card: **carte de crédit** (kahr-tuh duh cray-dee) f

cup: **tasse** (tahs) f

dance: **danser** (dahn-say)

dark: **foncé** (fohN-say)

daughter: **fille** (fee-y) f

day: **jour** (zhoor) m

delighted: **enchanté** (ahN-shahN-tay)

dentist: **dentiste** (dahN-teest) m

department store: **grand magasin** (grahN mah-gah-zanN) m

dessert: **dessert** (deh-sehr) m

doctor: **docteur** (dohk-tuhr) m

door: **porte** (pohrt) f

dress: **robe** (rohb) f

drink: **boire** (bwar)

drive: **conduire** (kohn-dweer)

ear: **oreille** (oh-rehy) f

easy: **facile** (fah-seel)

eat: **manger** (mahn-zhay)

e-mail address: **adresse électronique** (ah-dreh-say-lehk-tro-neek) f

employee: **employé** (ahN-plwa-yay) m

end: **fin** (fahN)

engineer: **ingénieur** (aN-zhay-nyuhr) m

even: **même** (mehm)

exit: **sortir** (sor-teer)

expensive: **cher** (shehr)

eye: **œil** (uhy) m

face: **figure** (fee-gewr) f

father: **père** (pehr) m

finger: **doigt** (dwah) m

finish: **finir** (fee-neer)

first name: **prénom** (pray-nohN) m

fish: **poisson** (pwa-sohn) m

flight: **vol** (vohl) m

flower: **fleur** (fluhr) f

flu: **grippe** (greep) f

foot: **pied** (pyeh) m

fork: **fourchette** (ewn foor-sheht) f

friend: **ami** (ah-mee) m

friend: **amie** (ah-mee) f

fruit: **fruits** (lay frwee) m

girl: **fille** (feey) f

give: **donner** (do-nay)

glass: **verre** (vehr) m

go: **aller** (ah-lay)

good: **bon** (bohN)

good bye: **au revoir** (ohr-vwahr)

good day: **bonjour** (bohN-zhoor)

good night: **bonne nuit** (bohN ne-wee)

good night: **bonsoir** (bohn-swahr)

grandchildren: **petits-enfants** (puh-tee-zahN-fahN)

granddaughter: **petite-fille** (puh-teet-feey) f

grandson: **petit-fils** (puh-tee-fees) m

green: **vert** (vehr) m

grocery store; general store: **épicerie** (ay-pees-ree) f

guitar: **guitare** (gee-tahr) f

hand: **main** (mahn) f

hat: **chapeau** (shap-oh) m

have: **avoir** (ah-vwahr)

he: **il** (eel) m

help: **aider** (eh-day)

hi: **salut** (sah-lew)

high school teacher; college professor: **professeur** (pro-feh-suhr) m

him: **lui** (lew-ee) m

holidays: **fêtes** (feht) f

house: **maison** (meh-zohN) f

how: **comment** (koh-mahN)

husband: **mari** (mah-ree) m

hungry: **faim** (faN)

I: **je** (zhuh)

ice cream: **glace** (glahs) f

illness: **maladie** (mah-lah-dee) f

in the back: **au fond** (o fohN)

introduce: **présenter** (pray-zahN-tay)

jacket: **veste** (vehst) f

jeans: **jean** (dzheen) m

knife: **couteau** (koo-to) m

large: **large** (lahrzh)

last name: **nom** (nohN) m

late: **en retard** (ahn ruh-tahr)

lawyer: **avocat** (ah-vo-kah) m

leave: **partir** (pahr-teer)

light-colored: **clair** (klehr)

like; love: **aimer** (ay-may)

live: **habiter** (ah-bee-tay)

lunch: **déjeuner** (day-zhuh-nay) m

madam; missus: **madame** (mah-dahm) f

man's suit jacket: **veston** (vehs-tohN) m

me: **moi** (mwa)

meal: **repas** (ruh-pah) m

meat: **viande** (vyahnd) f

mild: **doux** (doo)

miss: **manquer** (mahn-kay)

mister: **monsieur** (muh-syuh) m

modern: **moderne** (moh-dehrn)

money: **argent** (ahr-zhahn) m

mother: **mère** (mehr) f

mountain: **montagne** (mohn-tahn-yuh) f

must: **devoir** (duh-vwahr)

napkin: **serviette** (sehr-vyeht) f

narrow: **étroit** (ay-trwah)

neck: **cou** (koo) m

next day: **lendemain** (lahN-duh-mahN) m

next to: **à côté de** (ah ko-tay duh)

nice; beautiful: **beau** (bo)

noisy: **bruyant** (bree-ahn)

nose: **nez** (nay) m

not at all: **pas du tout** (pah dew too)

now: **maintenant** (man-tuh-nahN)

nurse: **infirmier** (aN-feer-myay) m

ocean: **mer** (mehr) f

of course: **bien sûr** (byan sewr)

office: **bureau** (bew-ro) m

okay: **ça va** (sah vah)

on the left: **à gauche** (ah gosh)

on the right: **à droite** (ah drwaht)

on time: **à l'heure** (ah luh)

on; on top of: **sur** (sewr)

one: **un** (uhN)

one-way (ticket): **aller-simple** (ah-lay-sahnpl) m

only: **seulement** (suhl-mahN)

orange: **orange** (or-ahnzh) f

outside: **dehors** (duh-ohr)

over there: **là-bas** (lah-bah)

passport: **passeport** (pahs-pohr) m

peas: **petits pois** (puh-tee pwa) m

people: **personnes** (pehr-sohn) f/pl

pepper: **poivre** (pwavr) m

perfect: **parfait** (pahr-feh)

phone number: **numéro de téléphone** (new-may-ro duh tay-lay-fohn) m

physician: **médecin** (mayd-saN) m

piano: **piano** (pee-ahn-oh) m

picture: **photo** (foh-toh) f

plate: **assiette** (ah-syeht) f

play: **jouer** (zhoo-ay)

police: **police** (poh-lees) f

pork: **porc** (pohr) m

potatoes: **pommes de terre** (pohm duh tehr) f

pound (weight): **livre** (leevr) f

prefer: **préférer** (pray-fay-ray)

pretty: **joli** (zho-lee)

put: **mettre** (meh-truh)

raincoat: **imperméable** (an-pehr-may-ahbl) m

raw vegetables: **crudités** (krew-dee-tay) f

red: **rouge** (roozh)

retired person: **retraité** (ruh-treh-tay) m/f

return (something): **rendre** (rahndr)

round trip: **aller-retour** (ah-lay-ruh-toor) m

salt: **sel** (sehl) m

saucer: **soucoupe** (soo-koop) f

seat: **siège** (syehzh) m

secretary: **secrétaire** (suh-cray-tehr) m

see: **voir** (vwahr)

see you soon: **à bientôt** (ah byan-to)

see you tomorrow: **à demain** (ah duh-man)

sell: **vendre** (vahndr)

she: **elle** (ehl) f

shirt: **chemise** (ewn shuh-meez) f

shoe size: **pointure** (pwan-tewr) f

shoulder: **épaule** (ay-pohl) f

show: **montrer** (mohN-tray)

sister: **soeur** (suhr) f

skirt: **jupe** (zhewp) f

slacks: **pantalon** (pahN-tah-lohN) m

sleep: **dormir** (dor-meer)

small; short: **petit** (puh-teet)

sneakers: **baskets** (bahs-keht) f

snow: **neige** (nehzh) m

soccer: **football** (fewt-bahl) m

soccer (Canada): **soccer** (soh-kehr) m

something: **quelque chose** (kehl-kuh shoz)

son: **fils** (fees) m

speak; talk: **parler** (pahr-lay)

spoon: **cuillère** (kwee-yehr) f

stay: **séjour** (say-zhoor) m

stay: **rester** (rehs-tay)

stop: **arrêt** (ah-reh) m

store: **magasin** (mah-gah-zan) m

strawberry: **fraise** (frehz) f

street: **rue** (rew) f

sugar: **sucre** (sewkr) m

suitcase: **valise** (vah-leez) f

sun: **soleil** (soh-lehy) m

supermarkets: **supermarché** (sew-pehr-mahr-shay) m

sweater: **pull** (pewl) m

sweatshirt: **sweat** (sweet) m

swimming: **natation** (nah-tah-see-ohN) f

take: **prendre** (prahndr)

tea: **thé** (tay) m

teaspoon: **cuillère** (kwee-yehr) f

telephone; call: **téléphoner** (tay-lay-foh-nay)

thank you: **merci** (mehr-see) m

that one: **celui-là** (suh-lwee-lah) m

that one: **celle-là** (sehl-lah) f

then: **puis** (pew-ee)

there is: **il y a** (ee-lee-yah)

they: **elles** (ehl) f

they: **ils** (eel) m

think: **penser** (pahN-say)

thirsty: **soif** (swaf)

this one: **celui-ci** (suh-lwee-see) m

this one: **celle-ci** (sehl-see) f

ticket: **billet** (bee-yeh) m

tie: **cravate** (krah-vaht) f

tip: **pourboire** (poor-bwar) m

tired: **fatigué** (fah-tee-gay)

today: **aujourd'hui** (o-zhoor-dwee)

tomato: **tomate** (to-maht) f

too bad: **tant pis** (tahN pee)

too much: **trop** (tro)

town: **ville** (veel) f

train: **train** (trahn) m

train station: **gare** (gah) f

travel: **voyager** (vwah-yazhay)

trunk: **coffre** (kohfr) m

two: **deux** (duh)

underpants: **slip** (sleep) m

until: **jusqu'à** (zhews-kah)

veal: **veau** (vo) m

vegetables: **légumes** (lay-gewm) m

vendor: **marchand** (mahr-shan) m

wait: **attendre** (ah-tehn-druh)

waiter: **serveur** (sehr-vuhr) m

wallet: **porte-monnaie** (pohrt-moh-neh) m

want: **vouloir** (voo-lwahr)

warm; hot: **chaud** (sho)

watch: **regarder** (reh-gahr-day)

watch: **montre** (mohntr) f

water: **eau** (lo) f

we: **nous** (noo)

wear: **porter** (pohr-tay)

week: **semaine** (suh-mehn) f

weird; bizarre: **bizarre** (beez-ahr)

what: **qu'est-ce que** (kehs-kuh)

when: **quand** (kahN)

where: **où** (oo)

which: **quelle** (kehl)

white: **blanc** (blahn)

who: **qui** (kee)

why: **pourquoi** (poor-kwa)

wide: **large** (larzh)

wife: **femme** (fahm) f

win: **gagner** (gahn-yay)

window: **fenêtre** (fuh-nehtr) f

wine: **vin** (van) m

wool: **laine** (lehn) f

work: **travailler** (trah-va-yay)

yard: **jardin** (zhahr-daN) m

yellow: **jaune** (zhon)

you: **toi** (twa)

you (formal): **vous** (voo)

you (informal): **tu** (tew)

zip code: **code postal** (cohd pohs-tahl) m